Freshwater Press, USA

As My Soul Prospers is Book 3 of a 4-book series: **Don't Refuse Me, Lord.**

> **Don't Refuse Me, Lord,** Book 1
>
> **Lord, Help My Debt,** Book 2
>
> **As My Soul Prospers,** Book 3
>
> **Don't Work for Money,** Book 4

ISBN# 978-1-893555-87-7

Paperback Version

Table of Contents

As My Soul Prospers

Freshwater Press, USA

Character Flaws

Who you are will become blatantly apparent when you have *means* to express it.

You've known a number of people who were wonderful, kindhearted, even meek until they came into *their own,* until they moved into lucrative careers or received inheritances. Or, they may have finally finished years and years of professional schooling. They finally got their long-desired and long-deserved promotion or moved into *their* ministry. Once they come into their-- *whatever*, they become what seems like a completely different person. Now that they can finance things they really want to do, they do them. Now that they can afford certain clothes, they dress differently. Now that they have a platform from which to speak or prestige and authority to wield, they talk differently and walk past people whom they've leaned on or used to be their best friends in the lean days of the past. Now that they've attained what seems like their lifelong goals, they should be celebrating and serving God all the more, but they've become obnoxious.

Now that you have means, a forum, a way to express what is really in **you**, that's what you will *express*. You haven't *become* it; you were always *that*. It was hidden by poverty or the lack of means. But now that you finally have what you need, *you do what you want to do!* All those years of sacrifice, being bossed around and told what to do are over. Now it's your turn!

Now begins your reign of terror.

As ugly as it is,

poverty covers a multitude of ugly.

Have you ever noticed that it seems to take a long time to get some things from God--

even the things that *He* promised you--, stuff you may not have even asked for. You've been waiting for years, haven't you? Abraham waited 24 years for the child that God promised. What's God doing? Why is He taking so long?

God is developing your character.

He is perfecting and maturing you. So when you get that promise, that power, that ministry, that money, that family, that career, He will be able to **trust** you with it. God doesn't put power in the hands of the ungodly, the untrustworthy, the childish, immature, or the reckless. But they may try to circumvent God and steal it. God doesn't place promotion on a person before they are ready. He takes you step by step through your own character and spiritual development, so:

- He can trust you.
- He can trust that you know how to hear His voice and be obedient to Him.
- You can accept each step of the way. God will take you to the next level when you are ready.

He will not force anything on you.

- You can trust *yourself* with the Promise. God knows you already. He knows your heart and your ways. Sometimes going through tests and trials is the way you learn about *yourself,* your tendencies, and the true you that's in there.

As ugly as it is, poverty can cover a multitude of ugly, but that's no reason to stay poor. Cultivating the Fruit of the Spirit works out character flaws so you can be beautiful inside and out, and prosperous.

Money can be such a temptation; now that formerly clean and good people can *afford* drugs, they use drugs. Of course no one can afford drugs--, only the wise know that. All of a sudden tee-totalers are using alcohol. How many times have you heard folks say things like: *When I start working? When I grow up? When I finish school, when I get my own money, job or apartment...?* That's why God hasn't let so many people get to the places *they* have planned for themselves. Because once they get there, they would only destroy themselves. That's love and Mercy that God won't let you self-destruct because of your *I-want's, I-need's, I have-to-haves, and now I-can-affords.*

I think about a longtime friend, Marvin, who I no longer recognized since he became successful. I asked God, *Did you make that?*

God responded. ***I framed it. Then I gave Marvin two crayons, one called success and the other prosperity. I formed and framed it. But when Marvin received his crayons, he colored it. He colored outside the lines. Marvin is not what I intended him to be.***

Could this be why God seems to be refusing you? Could it be for your own good; until you prosper in your soul, working out character flaws? The world says that if you get too much too soon, it'll burn you up. That may mean, like Lucifer, you may go to or get too close to hell if you try to ascend too fast.

As God has prospered you, and you've grown in finances as well as prestige, authority, and popularity, what have you done with it?

What have you done with the power? How is it being expressed through you? What have you done for God and for the Kingdom of Heaven? The Word says that there are many gifts, but different administrations. You don't have to be like and weren't made to be like anybody else. But how are you *administering* your gifts and the things with which God has prospered you?

And, to motive, *why* do you want the things you are asking God for, really?

Finally, I'm Somebody

Let's say you're not one of *those* people. You're a good and decent Christian who God has finally blessed. You just got a major promotion at your job. The Kingdom of Hell may be glad you got a promotion too. The devil is smart enough to know that he may be able to accomplish more through a manager, a president, or the owner of a company than through the mail clerk.

If you progressed on God's schedule, you'd would have been selected in your *season*.

In your season you'd be matured and prospered emotionally, intellectually and moving in God's will. However, when you are determined to push forward trying to pass God to get advances and promotion, Satan may help you get ahead. Coming up too fast can be the cause of a man's downfall. Anyway, the devil may help you by getting rid of your former *demonized* manager who gave you the past 15 years of on-the-job grief. Satan is through with your former manager anyway; the devil got all he could get out of that deceived loser. However, if you've pushed past God to self-promotion, you'll most likely be ahead of your *season*. You'll be sour and green like so many unripe apples.

If you could read the job assignments the Devil's got planned for you, you might be surprised. Would you be prepared? He wants you walking in prideful, lustful flesh. Now that you **think** you *arrived* by your own efforts, now that you think you're somebody, there's surely going to be temptations. All that pride you have in yourself for earning *your* promotion is the open door for the devil.

But God allowed it. God has allowed you to arrive at this new position, and now if you walk after the Spirit and not after the flesh, you can be victorious to the glory of God. Whatever the devil has planned for you, the evil, torment, torture, disappointments and devastation, God has planned success and means of escape from devil traps, for your good. The danger is that if your soul (character) is not prospered, the position, pay, power and all it's perks may go to your head. This is why one needs to prosper in their soul before they receive great rewards and successes, both spiritually and in the natural.

Don't disappoint God. You know that when you give your child new gifts, new responsibilities, and permission to do something new, something more, you really want them to succeed. God also wants you to succeed. If ugly is in you, get it out before it destroys you and the work that God has planned to accomplish through you. Then go ahead, walk in that God-given success and prosperity.

Idol *gods*

Idle, idol "*gods*" will bring out things in you that should not be in you in the first place. Those *gods* will bring out character flaws that manifest as selfish ambition and works of the flesh. These are not appealing to God and will not bring Him to your *situation*. When you have means to express yourself fully, you may find that you live in selfishness, enviousness, bitterness, pride, deceit, unforgiveness. Until people get what they want out of other people and situations, even out of God, they may be nice, nice, nice. Then all of a sudden when they have their comeuppance they become obviously and blatantly *who they are*. I don't think people become other than what they are. I think who they are **surfaces**. Those who *appear* rich or successful but act in vanity, hatred, malice and pride were always that way. It just may not have been previously expressed. I've never heard anyone say that money makes you mean; I'm pretty sure the individual was already mean, it just hadn't been expressed yet.

Marvin never used to hang out in clubs and bars until after he finished school. In school, Marvin was under the pressure of making the grades. Marvin used to pray and go to church--, whenever he had an upcoming exam. Marvin never used to dress like *that*. Marvin never used to wear his hair like that. Marvin was such a nice young man. No he wasn't. Marvin didn't have any money when he was in school. But now that Marvin is earning 6 figures, he can *express* himself--, both who he thinks he is and who he wants to be. The same Marvin who was saved all through college and law school is now wild because of money. Girls are attracted to the painfully shy Marvin--, or at least attracted to his money and cars. Now he has become a party animal. In reality, Marvin was never shy. That was insecurity because he didn't think he had **enough** to fit in or *belong*.

A person who has become miserly and cheap now that they have money and status is different, but no different. Money, status, and pride are some of the things that bring out ugly, flesh works. Money exerts a certain pressure, and even more pressure if you've exalted it to a *god*. Under pressure, what's in you will come out.

Don't refuse me, Lord; Lord, help me may be your cry. God's answer... ***As your soul prospers, I will promote you.***

God refuses ugly, fleshy requests every day of the week, every hour of the day. That's why it's taking so long for God to bless you. He is maturing your character--, your soul.

Exercise:

1. Repent of character flaws, and fleshiness.
2. What are my character flaws that I see in myself?
3. What are my character flaws that people have told me about myself?
4. What has God spoken to me about my character?
5. What things do I need to change?
6. List the flaws that are in more than one category.
7. Which will you work on 1st? When do you plan or hope to be over your first flaw?
8. How will you work on these flaws? What is your plan?

9. What kind of help will you ask for in order to make these changes?
10. Will you seek help from other people?

From God?

From the Holy Spirit?

Humility is having an accurate assessment of yourself, your character, your need for repentance and correction. Whatever you need to repent of, do it sincerely and with a broken spirit and pureness of heart. This way God can help you. He does not refuse the humble, those of broken spirit and a contrite heart, (Psalm 51:17).

In My Father's House

In my father's house there are many mansions
if it were not so. I would have told you.
John 14:2

John the Divine saw a vision of Heaven that he relates to us in the Book of the Revelation. Heaven is my Father's house. What's in that House and what's it like? Who's there and what are they doing? Here's a clue.

Whatsoever you bind on Earth shall be bound in heaven. What you lose on Earth shall be loosed in heaven.(Matthew 18:18)

If what is bound on Earth is also bound in Heaven, and what is loosed on Earth is loosed in Heaven--, then, are Heaven and Earth the *same*? Are they a replica of one another? They should be.

Which one came first, Heaven or Earth? Heaven. So Heaven, which we don't see, brings to manifestation what we do see in Earth. That which is spiritual, brings forth that which is natural. That which is unseen, brings to Earth that which is seen. That's what God did in Creation.

Then we asked the question, are we in order? What does our model, which is Heaven, look like? The answer to that question is the same as what should our Earthly mansion look like? Is our Earthly mansion in order so it can bring forth the right things on Earth? When I speak of mansion here, I mean our houses we live in and our natural bodies.

If we are called to be wise stewards, then whose house are you living in? God's. Everything belongs to God. Therefore the House we live in should be a replica of God's

House. Let's look above and see how we should be living.

Gates

There are 12 gates of Pearl at the entrance to Heaven. Twelve is the number of Government. Gates are counsel. We should be receiving and giving sufficient and wise counsel in our homes, to our spouse, our children and all who enter there. A visitor should be able to sense the presence of God when entering your home. Many visitors to my house, saved and unsaved, didn't really want to leave, but they didn't know why. It's the presence of God.

Your home should exemplify a Godly mansion here on Earth.

Twelve is the number of tribes in the Old Testament, the number of Disciples in the New Testament and the number of Elders in the Throne Room. Twelve is sufficiency; it is government. You should have a House sufficient for your needs and ministry, as necessary and ordained by God.

Cast not your pearls to swine. (Matthew 7:6)

As you are to give and receive counsel, do not cast your Wisdom to swine. Guard what goes out and guard what comes in your spiritual and natural *house*.

As the pearls are for the gates, guard your gates. What are your personal gates? Simply the openings in your temple, your body, the apertures that allow sight, hearing, taste and speech. Guard your heart with all diligence for out of it flow the issues of life, (Proverbs 4:23). Ordain your ear gates with pearls of Wisdom. Guard what you hear, what you say, what you eat, what you put in your house, and what you touch. You must do it yourself. Guard whatever goes in or through the paired and single orifices of your body.

No Demons Invited

And he said unto them, I beheld Satan as lightning fall from heaven. Luke 10:18

Nothing demonic or evil on us or in us can enter into Heaven, (Galatians 5). Neither should you be allowing evil *spirits* to enter your home if you are attempting to make a replica of God's House. Spirits are invisible. So you should not be inviting any into your home or allowing them in.

If you can't be spiritually sensitive, then be spiritually aware. You can ask the Holy Spirit, *"How is the atmosphere in here?"* Over time you will receive spiritual discernment. Then you will be able to take authority over uninvited and unwelcomed *spirits*. If you kick them out using the name of Jesus, they will fall *like lightning* into the pit of hell.

You might be saying, what can I do about this *evil-spirit* thing? You open the gates or the doors of your home by your behavior and actions. Either sinful or righteous behavior, attitudes and actions open the corresponding doors. When you argue, you invite a *spirit of division* or *contention* into your home. When you bring pornographic material into your home or by any route, magazines, television, or the Internet, you invite *lusting, adulterous demons* into your living space. Those demons really want to live *in* you, but they'll work around you, influence you as long as they can, hoping for an opportunity to invade an infest. Demons will stay until:

- Cast out, and/or
- You submit completely to God and resist them.

But first you must be aware of their presence, their existence, and persistence.

When you bring home something accursed, (stolen or hot), you opened the door for *lying* and *thieving spirits*. When you entangle or even think on works of the flesh, anything unclean, you open doors. None can come in except you open the door, or someone in your ancestral line has opened the door. If it's a generational demonic association or oppression or stronghold, an ancestor opened the door. Either way, you need to pull it down if your house is to be a replica of God's House.

Further, you should respect other people's houses. It is downright rude to bring your evil spirits into another's house. I threatened to put a plaque at my door that read:

Evil spirits not welcome. Please park your demons at the door if you want to enter here, or else stay outside with them.

Prayer

Let there be sweet smelling odors to God. Your prayers are the poetic incense of which the Bible speaks. Praying just when there's food on the table is for the lazy and the foolish. Little and temporal good is the sanctified plate of food in a cursed environment, going into a cursed body. Don't let supper time praying deceive you into thinking that you have a *relationship* with God. If your children only talk to you at mealtime, if they only stop what they were doing to eat, you wouldn't have a very good relationship with them. You wouldn't know them very well. And probably wouldn't understand their conversation. You might not recognize them, actually. If you are only praying at mealtime, you need to consider your motives toward God.

Being slack in prayer might be why so many sinners, seekers and even some saved folks, start prayers with: *Lord, it's me, Louis.*

They identify themselves to God because they know they don't have a **relationship** with Him. They don't know God, and they are not sure if God knows them. If they thought that God knew or was paying attention to them, they might not do all the things they do. If your children were this way, you'd certainly wouldn't care if they had an allowance, nice clothes, or a car to drive or any of the things children and teenagers want. God is the same about the things you want.

In that He seems to be refusing to give you what you ask for or need, then ask yourself, how's your relationship with Him? Can He? Should He? Not spending time with God is more like you're refusing *Him* instead of the other way around.

In God's Throne Room there is constant prayer. The Bible says to pray without ceasing (1 Thessalonians 5:17). In my Father's House that is the way it is according to Scripture. Further, the Bible reads, *As for me and my house, we will serve the Lord,* (Joshua 24:15c). Make your house like the Father's House as much as it is possible. Glorify God on Earth in your home and your physical body.

Value

You value your children, so you buy them gifts. God knows how to give even better gifts than you do, but when a child sees something of greater perceived value, that child will throw down that thing that's in his hand to get the new thing.

When a person sees something more desirable, they will drop what they are holding in their hand in hopes of acquiring the thing of greater value. Not greedy adults. They want *both* the old and the new. That's not Biblical and it won't work. That's the *spirit of greed* in operation. Throw down tithes, offerings, alms. Throw the money at the feet of Jesus at the feet of the priest. Throw down the world's gold at your feet and **pave** your street of gold so you can walk on what God walks on. Put down the old and acquire the better thing. If anyone has not yet dropped the *gold*, it may be because they have not yet seen God, I mean really met and seen God.

Deadly Silence

The four and 20 elders fall down before him
that sat on the throne, and worship him that
liveth forever and ever, and cast down their
crowns before the throne, saying, thou art
worthy, O Lord, to receive glory and honor
and power, for thou hast created all things
for thy pleasure. They are and were created
(Revelations 4:10)

The lifting up of holy hands signifies
surrender. It shows that you have no weapons,
nothing in your hands that could hurt anyone. It
shows God that there is nothing that you would
rather hold in your hands or do with your hands
than simply lift them to worship Him. When
you **see** God, you would be willing to let go of

anything and everything that's in your hands to worship Him. If you know Him, if you understand the value of His love, you realize that whatever you've been trying to hold on to cannot compare. If you let go of the thing of lesser value, then you will have hands free to lift up to God. Throw down whatever is in your hand, whatever is of earthly value, to worship Him. This way *you* put **value** on your worship.

Silence

Silence is not necessarily golden. It can be deadly. Four beasts worship, saying *Holy, holy, holy* night and day around the Throne of God. The only silence in Heaven was for about a half an hour when the Seventh Seal was opened, (Revelations 8:1-5).

We should have 24-hour worship in our home. The prince of the powers of the air is defeated by the sound of worship. Worship ushers in and keeps the presence of God. The one-half hour silence in Heaven at the opening of the Seventh Seal, which brought devastation to the Earth, should tell us something. When we are not worshipping God, when praise and worship are not emanating from our mouths, bodies, and our houses, something devastating may be happening.

God is not vain, but He only stays where He is welcome. Your worship welcomes Him and keeps Him present so He can *keep* you. Half an hour without worshipping God is too long, and it's long enough for a seal, a curse, or a devastation to be loosed, if God allows it.

Faith comes by hearing. Play teaching tapes, CD's, downloads, and worship music in your home and car. Faith comes by hearing. Record your own voice so you can hear it over and again. I recorded my mother's favorite Scriptures in the Book of Psalms and Proverbs in my own voice to give to her as a gift. Later I learned about this principle, so I made copies of the tape to play over and again in my own house. I believe God, and because God is in me, I believe me. Anyone else, everyone else, I'm getting to know by the Spirit, by their works, by their fruit, by the children of their decisions and their walk with Christ.

Faith comes by hearing. Just because you heard it on the news, or the television doesn't make it true. Because you saw it in a magazine or newspaper doesn't make it true either. And certainly if you heard through the Grapevine, it probably is very far from truth. Even Marvin Gaye and Gladys Knight and the Pips of worldly fame, knew to believe half of what you see and some and none of what you hear.

God says that faith comes by hearing, not truth by hearing. A liar, a gossiper, a womanizer, or a politician could be repeating falsehoods over and over that will never make them true. We need keen discernment.

Faith comes by hearing, so when I say something, I believe that I will keep my own word. This is why **I practice being faithful**, so I will believe myself all the time.

Practicing the worship of God builds my faith for who He is, and when we have faith, He will reveal Himself to us. That revelation of Himself is in His presence, and we want His presence.

Order & Submission

In the Book of the Revelation, the 24 Elders laid down their gold crowns to worship God, (Revelations 4:4). The others submit to God's authority and order. Just as the order in the home is to submit to God and each other. The adults in the home are under authority. They are in order, therefore the children in the home are also under submission, authority and in order. In my Father's House, things are done decently and in order (1 Corinthians 14:40). I seek to emulate this as much as possible in my home.

Light

We also have. We have also a more sure word of prophecy, where until you do well, that you take heed as unto a light that shineth in a dark place, until the day dawn and the day star arise in your hearts. (2 Peter 1:19)

There is no need of light, for God giveth light. In my Father's House, the light that leads the way is of God. God is acknowledged in all the ways, and He directs the path. There's no one trying to outshine God.

And I will give him the morning Star

Revelations 22:8

Water

There's a river flowing from the Throne. Out of our belly shall flow rivers of Living Water, (John 7:38) folks that come to your house should be able to receive a Word in season.

Healing

There's a Tree of Life in Heaven with leaves on it for healing of the nations, (Revelations 22:2). He sent His Word and healed them (Psalm107:20). Words can heal. The prayer of faith can heal. In my Father's House doesn't just mean the church, it also means the home you live in, as well.

Folks should be getting healed in your house. You, your spouse, your children, and whomever may come to visit. There's healing and laying on of hands and there are gifts of healings. All these benefits are ours as we copy the Mansion, above.

This is our homework: ministry at home. The church part is our act of worship and fellowship. We don't have to go to church just to do ministry unless we live alone and there's no one to minister to there. Jesus said His House shall be called a House of Prayer. Church is for worship, prayer, fellowship and the equipping of the saints for Ministry. Once equipped, ministry should flow wherever you are, whenever ministry is needed. You shouldn't have to call your pastor because your child has a cold or a fever. Jesus' Disciples only called Him when everything they could do had no effect. You should be able to minister all, most of, at least some kind of healing in your home.

If you're not using your house for godly things, no wonder it is not as nice as it could be--, the atmosphere and the physical structure itself.

Power

My Father's House? There's fullness of joy because He is present. He's represented. He is revered. He is worshipped. He is adored. He is blessed. He is obeyed and honored. Where He is, there's power.

Don't refuse me, Lord. Then make your home a place where God would love to come to. Make your home a replica of Heaven by binding and *loosing* to make your home look like Above. Then all your needs will be supplied in the Order, in the Light, in the Praise, in the Worship, in the Counsel, in the Healing by the Power of Jesus Christ.

Exercise: My house spiritually and naturally.

11. Are your gates guarded? How so?

Spiritual entrance. What do you allow an invite in your House?

Prayer. When does prayer happen in your house? What kind of prayer?

The value, what value is placed on God in your house?

Worship goes on in my house--, when?

Order, submission, and authority-- is my house in order?

Are you under *submission*?

Do we obey **authority**, natural, civil and spiritual?

Do we have spiritual **Light** in our house? How do we know?

Water. Living water-- Is that in my house?

Healing. Can people or have people been healed in my house?

My family's health. How is it for those who live in my house?

Power - Is the power of God evident in my house? How so?

War In Your Members

From whence come wars and fightings
among you? Can they not hands? Even of
your lusts that war in your Members, you lust
and have not. You kill and desire to have and
cannot obtain. You fight in war, yet you have
not, because you ask not. James 4:1-2

We want so much from God. We want
the things that make us happy, comfortable and
things that we think make us look good. We
want nice houses, shiny cars and good paying
jobs that we only have to work two days out of
a week, if that. We want the perfect home and

the ideal work environment. We want the perfect spouse and perfect kids. We want a well-toned, healthy, fat-defying body that is invincible and impermeable by calories as we heap them on in the form of cheesecake and potato chips. Let's face it, we want it all.

Warring in our members? What's all the fighting about? That's just what the fighting is about. All the things we want are because someone else has those things, and because that someone else who has those things is making those things look good and desirable. The fighting is about:

- Not having those things.
- Wanting those things.
- That someone else has those things we like or feel as though we should have them.

The war in our members is against our brothers because of covetousness, envy, jealousy, and other works of the flesh. *Things* is not just material stuff, I'm talking about intangible items too, such as the **talents** that individuals have. How many people do you know in the local church choir, for example, who get along with everyone? I'm even unfortunately talking about the gifts of the Spirit that God bestows on whomever He wills. Jealousy and envy causes people to want the quality or ability that the talented or gifted person has.

In the Book of Acts, there was a man who asked that hands be laid on him so that he could have certain gift/power so he could profit from that gift. Some people's *profit* is money, to some it's notoriety, fame or simply attention.

Insecurity or egotism may cause the person with the gift to become hostile and antagonistic--, adding to the warring. Pharaoh and Herod were evil, insecure rulers who wanted to do away with anything that threatened their positions--, even babies. This could be why many don't try to win souls and bring new members to their church; they are guarding their own positions. People, when you're in your right position, nobody can move you out of it--, no principality, no power, nor any new member. Nobody but you.

Like too many, Saul became hateful and insecure when the new guy came. David and Saul could have worked together. It was on Saul; he was the senior member, he had the position, status and power. Saul was called of God, yet warred with David his successor. Saul could have had length of days and retired with glory and honour if he had treated David right. This is a fine example of what a person with no character and an unprospered soul will do with power or perceived threats to position and power.

As church infighting continues, God as our parent is looking on and is grieved that His creation can behave so Neanderthal and ignorant. As good parents you know if your two children are fighting and they both asked for cookies, which one will get the cookie? Neither of them. That's how God responds to warring brothers. Neither will be blessed until they make up. You may be smarter than you know, you got that from God. In the above example had David stooped to Saul's level, David wouldn't have been blessed either. So if you're the object of warring, maintain your righteousness and sin not.

Messing Up The Blessing

...one sinner destroys much, much good.
(Ecclesiastes 9:18b)

Warring with members in your local congregation could be messing up the blessing for you personally or, depending on who you are, your entire church. It could be blocking the flow of the corporate anointing. It could be negating so much powerful praise and worship in the House. It could be blocking the flow of revelation or the understanding and anointing that is to come from that revelation.

Further, it could be that if you're the one that's out of order, God will judge you and punish accordingly, in time. He says to agree with your adversary quickly. Seems to me if He has to step in, He may throw you in spiritual jail and you won't be receiving any blessings there. But the person you were warring with may be free and able to receive now that you've stopped harassing him.

After all that fighting, we are still praying up a storm, asking God for *things*. We plead, *Don't refuse me, Lord.* Then we sit back with amnesia of a sort and wonder why we don't get those *things*. We're asking God for things because living well is the best revenge, and you want to show that person that was irritating, teasing, picking at, aggravating, or tormenting you that you've got a special *relationship* with God, therefore <u>they</u> are wrong. You want to use God against them in your little flesh war, but it ain't gonna happen.

You may find comfort in things, and you may want to show that you live *large*. So part of the reason you are asking God for *things* is to heap upon your own lust, just to show your enemies a thing or two. Then you wait and wonder, what's wrong with God? Why is He taking so long to reward you, doesn't He know how wonderful you are?

After all, the other person is out of order. It can't be you. *You've* been wronged. You've been hurt. Can't God see how much all of this is hurting **you**?

So much pride. Beloved, open up a window and air the room out, then let your soul prosper.

Yeah, ask and receive, not because you ask a miss that you may consume it upon your lust. (James 4:3)

Here's the problem. Not getting along with people in the Faith.

Therefore if thou bring thy gift to the altar, and there remembrance that thy brother hath ought against thee, leave there thy gift before the altar, and go that way first be reconciled to their brother, and then come and offer that gift. (Matthew 5:23-24)

If God won't accept your gift or your offering when you are not getting along with your brother, then, why would **give** you something while you are not getting along with your brother? God doesn't accept your gift to *Him* as long as you have made enemies of brothers in the faith. *I love You, Lord, but I can't stand her or I can't stand brother So-and-so; You just don't know what he did to me.* Listen to those excuses. God has heard them all before.

Forgive

What does forgiving have to do with anything? Forgiving has everything to do with everything. It is the basis of Jesus' entire ministry. If you don't get this, if you don't understand forgiveness, then you don't understand how the Kingdom of Heaven works.

What if I have already humbled myself and asked for forgiveness, but the other person is still acting stupid, you may ask? What if they want to keep the war going? Then you've done all you can do. You're not responsible for other people harboring hatred, resentment, unforgiveness or bitterness in their hearts, *even if **_you_** started it*. If you have gone to them sincerely and apologized, and continue to pray for them --, that's all you can do. You cannot put yourself in a position to try to *please* them into treating you right.

Like David to Saul, there was no more David could do to make peace with Saul. He had shown Saul mercy, respect, and honor for having been called of God, and he had shown Saul forgiveness over and over. My best advice is:

Pray for them.

Distance yourself from them, especially if real warring flares up in their company. If God allows it, you may have to encounter that person, for example, if you work in the same office. If you can't distance yourself from them, then put on the whole armor of God and do spiritual battle.

Forgive them anyhow. Don't talk about them to other people. Live and let live.

If you must talk about them, limit it to conversations with God.

Live your life. Pray for them some more. Pray for yourself that you're in order and beyond spiritual reproach.

What's in the House?

Have you ever considered that God may have already given you the parts that make up the *things* that you're asking for with instructions, assembly required? If you think about it, you have many parts to making your life work, spiritually and naturally. You have the Word, faith, prayer, spiritual warfare, Thanksgiving, praise, worship, sowing, and reaping, among other things. You have parts--, things that you can use all together, or on an *as needed* basis. At certain times you use certain things. For instance, there's a time to pray and there is a time to sing and there is a time to praise. There's another time to worship. It depends on how you want to approach God and what you want from Him or want to give Him as to what method you use. You can approach Him in a number of different ways. Prayers such as petition, Thanksgiving, adoration and supplication. You can approach in song, praise, worship, or you can approach in meditation. Use the method that suits your needs, purposes, and grace. For instance if you are not good at meditation, but you are good at prayer, until practice improves, you approach in prayer.

You may have prayed and prayed to God, called out to Him for a certain tangible something, but He may turn around and ask you, as the Old Testament Prophet asked the widow woman, *What have ye in your house?* If God is asking you this, the answer is that you do have something in your house. Although you might not know what it is, or that you have it, or that it has value. Yet, God asked to make you aware of that you have something so He can then instruct you on how to use it.

Many times in the Bible, the seeker was told to use common everyday things in common or uncommon ways to receive miracle blessings from God.

The little woman was in dire straits when her two sons were about to be taken from her to make up for the debts of her deceased husband. You also might be pleading to God that your own sons will not be taken away from you, but they will not be stolen by the streets, and by the temptations of life. The little woman responded to the man of God, *"A little oil."*

In those days oil was very valuable and could be used in as an exchange, medium, or currency.

The Prophet accepted her answer and then said to her, "Go borrow vessels and not a few."

When asked, the woman had to use something that she already had to help herself be blessed of God. Then she had to ***do*** something to help herself be blessed of God. First, she had to make her situation known either in a positive or negative way when she went to borrow those vessels from other people. Did she say I have need of the vessels because God is going to bless me with much? Perhaps

45

she asked by saying, God has blessed or will bless me with much. Or maybe she said, I really need God to bless me this much. It is obvious that she had never had that much blessing before; she'd never had that much oil before, else her husband wouldn't have left debts, and she wouldn't have had to borrow so many vessels. If she had enjoyed bounteous oil quantities before, she would already have a great store of vessels.

Because of all the borrowed vessels, everyone knew that something was up at the widow woman's house. If they were worried about her before, they certainly were worried now that she was acting crazy to borrow so many vessels for so little oil.

Shut The Door

The Scriptures say that God will shut doors that no man can open (Revelations 3:8). God sent the Word through the prophet and the little woman obeyed. She shut the door. She had to shut the door to shut out and probably shut up those noisy, nosy neighbors. She had a great and urgent need, and the Prophet of God told her to borrow vessels; that was all they needed to know.

Why? God tells you just what you need to know. The next thing the nosy neighbors would have done was to tell her *how* God was going to bless her, or how He wasn't going to bless her, or that she was crazy.

Shut the door.

They would have told her all about how she could or couldn't handle the vessels, what happened to those vessels in the past and how they doubted what she was doing, even if the Prophet of God told her a *thus saith the Lord.* Or they would have commented on whether or not he was a real prophet.

Shut the door.

And when God shuts the door, no one can open it, and in this case, no one did.

Obediently the widow woman poured and poured into the vessels, until the last vessel was filled. Then the oil stopped. She sold the oil, paid her debts, kept her sons, and lived off the rest.

If you have a debt staring at you, think of the envelope as a vessel. Borrow, not a few. Go and get them. Address them to your creditors. Keep addressing them, knowing that you will put payments in these envelopes--, as much as you can each week. Before you know it, God will work a miracle with you paying those debts, then a suddenly of God, and you've paid off the debts. He will work debt cancellation in your favor. Before you know it, the debt will be paid and you'll keep those things you've worked so diligently for, and debt free.

God blesses order. The making out of the envelopes and paying regularly requires discipline. It is what God deems bless-worthy. God won't refuse you. He will help you.

Empty Vessels

Spiritually, when we were living in sin and on our way to hell, GOD borrowed a vessel from Heaven. Jesus was His name. God filled the vessel with His Spirit, Grace, Mercy, Truth and Wisdom. Then God caused the contents of that vessel to flow from Him and through Him until our spiritual debt was paid.

Then He told us to go live off the rest.

And God still does that for mankind. He sends us to get empty vessels, the unsaved or the saved, but unfilled. Because of His love and grace toward us, He fills them with love, mercy, grace, truth, understanding, Wisdom, His Spirit and anointing. And when the last vessel is filled, the anointing will stop. God will not refuse you when you are asking Him to fill an empty vessel. How many vessels have you filled or helped to fill? God will not refuse if that vessel has been properly cleaned by the Blood of Jesus, Salvation and is Spirit-filled. Just as He didn't refuse the little widow woman, He will not refuse when you are asking for the thing that will cancel the debt and cause sons to be birthed and grow up to maturity in Him.

As the little woman physically helped fill these vessels with oil, God kept her and her sons *full*. You help fill His vessels; He will fill yours.

Don't refuse me, Lord. But do I have to go get any vessels?

Yes.

Do I have to do anything for you to help me? **Yes.**

And as you pour into those vessels, God will pour into you and provision will be made for you.

Do I have to go out there and borrow from people?

Yes.

Then you're going to know what kind of shape I'm in. Lord, do I have to?

Yes.

The same man hears and does. It is an act of faith. It may not look so sane to the natural unsaved man, but it is better to be *spiritually sane* than naturally correct in the eyes of man The Lord will honor your spiritual sanity and obedience. He will not refuse that.

Exercise:

12. What's in my house?

You're Over Your Limit

Don't refuse me, Lord, no matter what I'm asking, don't refuse me because it's me--, because I really need it, because this is a good cause. Because I just can't stop myself. Because this is so important, a matter of life and death. 'Cause--, just because. Please don't refuse me, Lord. And just in case you're not going to bless me, I guess I'll just keep this tithe because I really need it.—

But a certain man named Ananias and Sapphira, his wife, sold a possession and kept back part of the prize, his wife also being Privy to it and brought a certain part. And later that the Apostles feet (Acts 5:1-2).

Giving up the ghost is a fancy old English way of saying that Ananias dropped dead. What about his wife, Sapphira? Whatever happened to her? God has a special heart for widows. He has sustained, blessed and kept many.

Sapphira fell down straightway at his feet and yielded up the ghost (Acts 5:10a).

Sapphira dropped dead, too. God is no respecter of persons. If you're a widow or a prominent businessman with real estate holdings, if you withhold from Him, He has the right to allow you to just drop dead. Is this funny? No, this is serious. This is real life and real death.

The Cost

There's a cost to reaping but not sowing except when gleaning; it is the same as robbery. How do you expect to receive a paycheck at a company where you do not work? How do you expect to reap where you do not and have not sown? You may look at the offering and believe your church is financially well off. The surplus in any ministry is for ministry to the lost, those who do not know of Jesus Christ. The extra that is in the treasury is for seeking the lost, to minister to those downtrodden by life. It is for those who are just coming into Salvation and knowledge of Jesus. These people are on credit. They are on Grace. That credit was provided to us by Jesus Christ, by whose dying for our sins erased a multitude of debt.

The ministry, energy, the finances in any ministry are for seeking the lost and for the new Christians who need spiritual, emotional and financial handholding, for season.

The Credit

The credit Jesus effected had to be magnificent to offset the sins of the **entire world**. That means you and me were each saved *on credit*. We each partake of and use up a part of this magnificent credit. We come into the Kingdom *on credit*. We then go out and get lost souls *on credit*. We cannot ever *pay* for Salvation, but we pay what we ought to and give what we are led to give. And what we put in God multiplies it. Don't ever say that you don't like math, because if it weren't for multiplication, there would have been no credit left to get you saved. **The credit was created by the people who planted seeds in your**

Salvation, starting with Jesus and including those who watered, was all to your advantage as God gave the increase. These are the people who do the work, God's work. The credit created and continued on by those who know Him, have relationship, and are faithful is what is used to perpetuate and grow ministry.

You're Over Your Limit

This may be why sometimes it seems God is refusing you. *Your spiritual credit limit has been reached.* No more blessings without praying. No more having the Devourer rebuked without tithing. No more presence of God without worship and praise. No more answers and deliverance without spiritual warfare. It's time for you to do it yourself, to pull your own weight, spiritually. And it's time for you to do *works*. No more piggybacking and living off someone else's spiritual sweat. Moses is dead. Moses couldn't have gotten you *in* anyway as hard as he tried-- even giving his life.

Grandma is dead. Who's praying for you now? There comes a time when you just can't tag along anymore and glean the blessings from those who pray, from those who worship, and from those who intercede, fast, are obedient, and disciplined.

When you want your credit limit increased at the bank, you show that you have been disciplined and paying regularly, following all the rules that the bank has set forth. Have you got a Bible? Read it; those are the rules that God has set forth. Find out how to get more grace, more favor, more blessings. Be disciplined and regular. God has no shortage of blessings and favor. He won't refuse you if you prove that you're faithful and able to handle more.

The extras, the credit and the surpluses in ministries are not for those who are saved, been saved for years and just sitting in church doing nothing. The extras are to **win more souls** to the Kingdom and minister to baby Christians, *for a season*.

Extras are not to feed those who don't feel like bringing anything or are too selfish to bring anything to the worship, to the ministry. You're not supposed to look in the storehouse of the House of God and say, *They've got plenty, why should I bring anything in? It's just making that preacher fat.*

The overflow in the House of God is for ministry, and chances are about 100%, in your church, that is exactly what it's been used for.

Gleaning is for the poor, the lost, the unsaved. It is for those who don't have a field of their own, it is for those who don't know they *have a field of their own yet*. Gleaning is not for the saved, for those who have Covenant with God. Gleaning is not forever. It is for the season until you come into your own and make Covenant with God who is well able to bless you.

The tithe provides for you in better ways than leftovers. God wants to establish Covenant with you. *You* are supposed to provide gleaning substance for the indigent, **not picking it up for yourself**.

On to Glory

If you are saved, yet you are not going to participate in the salvation of others, then what are you doing, actually? If you're going to hinder ministry by taking away from the funds, the time and the energy that could be used on the Lord because of your greed, selfishness and disobedience, then you're really in the way.

You got yours; don't you care about the salvation and deliverance of others? If you don't, then what is your purpose right now? Folks active in ministry have work to do. Get out of the way and start doing your part. Start bringing your tithes and offerings into the House of God first. Then start doing some real Kingdom work instead of soaking up all the ministry for yourself.

God put gifts in you. Find out what your spiritual gifts are, what you enjoy doing and what God has called you to do instead of praying for Jesus to do it, or watching other church members doing it, you. **You do it**.

That's Not Your Field Of Corn

If you keep coming to fields of corn that you didn't plan in order to eat and become full, then you're stealing. Some of the Saved are coming to the House of God and taking all they can. They are not gleaning, because gleaning is for those who don't have but have permission to take. Those without permission are those are getting the food bank Thanksgiving basket who don't even need it are not gleaners, this smacks of stealing.

People who can afford to, but do not pay tithes and offerings but get all the perks the Church has to offer--, that's like taking Tupperware to the buffet and then sneaking out the side door without paying before the check comes. That's probably why they make you pay first at buffets. It's easier to sell food to the hungry man.

If you're a mature saint, you are supposed to plant your own fields, and not live on the leftovers of others. You are responsible and accountable for every field of corn that you did not plant or participate in planting, but that you've eaten from, because you're taking spiritual nourishment, and physical help out of that ministry. That same ministry could have sowed into or saved the lives of many more, bringing them into the Kingdom. But you took the incentive or support gift instead of a lost soul, as if you need to get saved all over again every month.

One Hen Planted

Let me remind you of the children's story, the **Little Red Hen**. The Little Red Hen found some seeds. Having Wisdom, she knew some things about seeds:

1. They were seeds.
2. They were wheat seeds, and that
3. They should be planted. That's just not chicken wisdom either, because she could have just eaten them; hens really liked to eat seeds.

The Little Red Hen asked all the farm animals, *"Will you help me plant these seeds?"* They all declined, having better things to do.

As the growing season passed, the hen was blessed with more Wisdom because she knew when it was time to harvest. When it was harvest time, the Little Red Hen asked the same question, *"Who will help me?"* All the animals checked their schedules. They were all too busy to go to the fields to harvest.

The Little Red Hen knew that seeds would grow, created a crop that she then harvested. Not being stopped, she set out to mill the harvested wheat into flour. Again, no other animals helped.

Now the final step. Generously the hen offered all the farm animals **in** after she had begun the Ministry of making bread with homegrown wheat, from scratch. No pun intended, since chickens really love to scratch.

Just like the Parable of the Penny, the hen offered everyone, anyone an opportunity to share equally in the reward, no matter what time in the process they started, just as Jesus has done for us whether we are saved at birth, as a teen, as a young adult, or if you get a clue and accept Jesus before you drop dead, you will inherit eternal life.

As in the Penny Parable all got a penny no matter what time of day they started. The only people who did not get a penny were those who **never started**. The only animals who did not get to have any bread once it was smelling good, were those who never joined in the work--, which was all of them except the Little Red Hen.

Both baking bread and ministries is <u>work</u>. It's a job that you accept in love and by faith. God pays you, not the preacher, not the church. Ministry can be very deceiving to the untrained and uninitiated, it looks as though you are working for others, but you are really ***working for yourself***, laying up good works for yourself in Heaven. Many saved and committed saints should gladly raise a sign that reads:

Will work because of Salvation.

In the Parable we are discussing, the one doing the hiring owned all the pennies. Anyone in the Parable who didn't work but still got a penny stole it. The Bible doesn't recount that, but it can be reasoned out. The Little Red Hen owned the bread. She was willing to share the bread, share the wheat, share the work, and divide the bread. But no one wanted to share in the *process*. They just wanted to partake of the progress. If any animal ate of that bread without the hen's permission, they stole it.

You are to pick up your cross and follow Jesus. You didn't have to take on the sin of the world to be saved, you didn't have to be crucified to receive eternal life, and you didn't have to go to hell, though you may have chosen to go through it in your unsaved escapades, but you have to share in some of the process. You have to do some work.

God owns the Bread of Life, and you are invited to the table. After partaking of it, after using part of that magnificent credit. You should gladly state:

I will work because of salvation. I will work because I truly value what I have received, and I will work because I want others to have this Bread.

After you receive, use what you received to bless others.

What if Jesus sought the face of God for 40 days and 40 nights and sat down on a pew and talked about how glorious His retreat was, but didn't do any *works* and did not **work**? You would think something was wrong with Him. Does that scenario sound familiar? No wonder God is refusing folk who run after conferences, seminars and retreats and do not work in any of their church's ministries.

Your pastor has been modeling *work* for you. He's not been doing it *for* you, or *instead* of you. He has not been doing it so you could find a comfortable pew, then brag to your friends about the ministries of your church or how wonderful your pastor is while you only profess to the choir how saved you are. Your pastor has been leading and showing you the way. Now you are to follow him as he follows Christ.

When you are repeatedly going to church knowing that there should be seed there, but you don't bring any in, then you are stealing. When you're repeatedly go to your church knowing that there is cultivating and work to be done to support the seed, but you don't, then that's a form of stealing. When you repeatedly go to receive of the Bread, but you never do anything to support the coming forth of that Bread, when you eat to your satisfaction; that is a form of stealing.

Don't refuse me, Lord, just keep feeding me no matter what I do or don't do. If I'm over the limit, Lord, won't you just *increase my limit*, please? That's not your prayer, is it?

Exercise:

13. Am I over the limit?
14. Gleaning- Have I reached my gleaning limit?
15. Giving- have I reached the limit in not giving? Not tithing? Not offering?
16. Have I gotten all the free stuff I can?
17. Have I gotten all the free stuff that I can, under the guise of favor?

18. In my prayer life, am I still living off grandma's prayers?

My spouse's prayers?

My mother's prayers?

The prayers of others?

Or do I have a regular, consistent, fervent prayer life of my own?

19. Am I contributing to others who may not know how to pray yet or may not have the discipline to pray regularly?

If so, named three people.

20. Am I over the limit in receiving God's blessings because of not working in ministry or in my church?
21. Am I praising God or am I living off the praise of the people in my church?
22. Am I living off other people's worship, or am I worshipping God regularly myself at my church and on my own? Be honest.
23. Do I have a worship life yet or am I still gleaning?
24. Am I interceding for the unsaved, those who are weaker in faith and cannot do spiritual warfare for themselves?

25. Am I extending spiritual credit to anyone else in any of the above categories as has been rendered to me, extended to me?
26. Who am I praying for?
27. What unsaved or undisciplined people am I standing in the gap for until they can stand on their own. And, even better, when will they be able to stand in the gap for another?

Humble Yourselves and Pray

If my people, which are called by my name,
shall humble themselves, and pray, and seek
my face and turn from their wicked ways,
then will I hear from the heavens or from
heaven, and will forgive their sin and will
heal their land.

2 Chronicles 7:14

How can we humble ourselves regarding
money and receive financial blessings of God?
Man is so proud about who he thinks he is and
the things he has. Humility is more pleasing to
God. The wise man realizes he doesn't have
anything. He realizes he is only a steward of
things he has. So many people have pride in
status, position, prestige and wealth. The Bible
says that pride cometh before destruction,

(Proverbs 16:18). So if we have too much pride in money and stuff, it's only a matter of time before the fall or destruction.

When you have sufficiency, you probably trust in that sufficiency. When you go to the store and you have cash to buy the things that you want or need, you trust in the cash you have in your pocket. You mentally add up all the things you're choosing to make sure you have enough money on you. If you have money in your checking account, then you make sure you have your check and driver's license so you can write a check. If you have a credit card, then you trust in your credit.

When having money, paper or plastic, many don't give God a thought and they simply choose the items they want to purchase. But when those things that you have trust in--, money, checks, credit cards have gone, then you start looking for another source. You may ask friends or family, but if they turn you down or fail you, after you get over your disappointment or anger with them, you may then seek God.

Some seek God before getting over soul offences and anger and then expect that God will not refuse us in that state. After all we justify in our minds, *we've* been offended. *We* need extra care. We think we are extra deserving. Plus we want to show those so and so's. That we can make it without them and their spare change. We want to show them that we can do fine without their input. How in the world do we think we are going to be doing fine when we needed them for a loan in the first place?

If family shuts you down, it is not because they hate you necessarily. It could be because you didn't pay them back last time; you're unfaithful. It could be because they really can't spare it, or they really don't have it. Then you should pray for them instead of being angry at them. It could be because their loaning or giving you money all the time isn't helping you or them. It could be that they are finally obeying God and **letting God be your source**. Then praise God for their obedience. It could be any number of reasons, but the reasons are theirs, not yours. You cannot decide what they should do with their money.

Even if you work for them as their accountant or financial consultant, you can make suggestions, but no matter who you are, you cannot tell them what to do.

Further, you shouldn't try to tell them what to do with their money, because you obviously don't know what to do with yours. You either have much less than they do, or your money management skills need work since you ran out of money before they did. And if you need a loan, you're probably not doing a good job as a steward.

Stop Here

Do I owe any family members money?
Do I owe any of my friend's money?
Have I lost friends because of unpaid personal loans?
What do I plan to do about any of the above?

Is More Better?

Nope. More is not necessarily better when it comes to money. Managing more money is not easier than managing less money. When you come to that realization, then you're ready for more money.

Do you trust in money? Test yourself.

Case 1

Rent is $1000 per month. The tithe is $150. You have $1500 available each month. And no other obligations. You can pay your tithe and even have $350 to spare after everything is paid to use any way you choose. No problem. All you need is discipline.

Case 2

What if you only have $1000 per month, and the tithe is $100. you have $1100 per month to pay the rent. Also no problem if you're disciplined and obedient, unselfish and not fearful. Pay your tithe, then pay your rent. Just pay it. You don't need any faith for that, just discipline to make out the check or money order and then take it, mail it or cash app it to the landlord. There's none extra. That takes discipline, love, obedience and courage.

Case 3

Rent is $1000 per month. You have $1000 income, and a tithe of $100. Do you pay your bills first or your tithe?

Which covenant did you make first, the one with God or the landlord?

If you couldn't afford the rent after paying the tithe, you lied on your lease application. That lease is invalid spiritually, but in the natural it is valid, and you're in the natural world right now. Who has ever calculated the tithe in anyone's expense column when applying for a loan or credit? No one that I know of. That's why we Christians should. You must put God first in your tithes and offerings, in your budget, and when planning your life in the real world. The landlord will wear you out until you pay your rental obligations, whereas God doesn't seem to be saying much about being robbed every month or week or whenever you get paid. So you acquiesce to the landlord, is that right?

The tithes should be paid first, even though the rent is probably due on the first. What do you do in this case? Which contract did you agree to first? Salvation or the rent? **Pay your first commitment first.** If the first commitment is not God, be faithful until God brings you to a place where you can pay Him first, now that you know better.

If you are not tithing as a Christian, you've got to make some changes. Say, God, I want to honor You. Show me how to pay my tithe and meet my obligations. Do I *give* my way out of this and into prosperity? Do I get a second job that does not interfere with serving You? Do I wait on job promotion? Do I cut back on my natural expenditures such as cable, snacks, and entertainment?

As you decide to honor God and pay your tithe first, not your credit card bill or a night out to dinner, you have just humbled yourself before God.

You are no longer Mr. Big Stuff to your landlord or your friends. You no longer pretend that you have it made in the shade. You've humbled yourself to trust and depend on God. **You've just humbled your money**. You have just humbled your money from being your provider, from being your *god*. You've just put money in its place, the offering basket. You've just put money in its proper position to bless you in the Kingdom of God.

We are not saying that your needs should not be provided for. God will not leave you out in the cold. Didn't He make a lush paradise for Adam and Eve? How much more is He willing to give you? After all, you have His Spirit in you, don't you? As the Scripture instructs now, all you have to do is seek God and pray.

Prayer

Don't refuse me, Lord. It's that I really do have a need. I want to trust You and honor You from now on. I repent of having trusted in cash, checks, credit cards, any form of money or finances. I repent of having trusted in other people. You are my God. You are my Savior; You are my source. Whether I can make purchases at the mall or not does not define who

I am, nor does it define the glory you put in me. It only entertains, pleases and comforts my flesh. Now when I humble myself, I humble my money. No longer haughty or prideful about what I have or who I think I am because of finances, I trust You, Lord, in the name of Jesus. I put you first. I pay the tithe, I give offerings and share with those less fortunate than myself. I put you first in my finances from this day forward and I know you will be faithful to bless me and keep me in Jesus' name. Amen.

Exercise:

Give a humbling gift over and above your tithe to God.

Give it at your next church service or mail it to a ministry that feeds you. Pray to God about it first. Ask Him what to give. Then ask God to do a work in you, believing Him, rather than money.

As My Soul Prospers

Beloved, I wish above all things, that thou may as prosper and be in health, even as thy soul prospereth.

3 John 1-2

We all want to prosper. We want gain, increase, and good health. But do we want our souls to prosper? What is a soul for that matter, and how does it prosper?

What is a soul?

… And the Lord God formed Man of the dust of the ground and breathed into his nostrils the breath of life. And the man became a living soul. Genesis 2:7

The soul comes from God. It is on loan to the human body. The spirit is the Breath of God. It is the thing that makes the living alive, while the temperament of the soul makes up the personality.

When God recalls the soul, that person is called home or said a different way, they die. Depending on if they are saved or not, and depending on what they've done with it, the soul will either go to Heaven or hell in the White Throne judgment.

Souls are God's creations. But the devil wants souls. The devil doesn't really want your money or your health. He wants to negatively affect your soul. **When you tie your soul to things and people, the devil touches you by touching those things and people**. The soul is from God, but the devil is trying to steal it from whomever he can tempt. It is stolen by trickery and deception. It is stolen by poor choices and bad decisions, such as choosing sin over holiness.

The Soul Lives

…And my soul shall live because of thee,
Genesis 12:13b

The soul is a living thing that lives in our clay body to give it Will, intellect and emotions, what we call personality. If our personality comes from God, shouldn't we be like Him? If our will, intellect and emotions come from God, shouldn't we all have Godly will, only wanting to do what God does? Yes. Shouldn't we be thinking like, or at least aspiring to think like God? And shouldn't our emotions be modeled after Him? Instead of the afternoon talk shows?

Yes, says the sane man. But there are many more variables and influences.

The Soul Departs

And it came to pass as your soul was in departing for she died that she called his name Benoni, but his father called him Benjamin. Genesis 35:18

The soul leaves when the flesh dies. Too often this is a result of acute or long-term sickness, disease, accident, or the body wearing out. The soul can depart because the Lord calls it home even while the flesh is fine, healthy, even young. The Lord may require one's soul, (Luke 12:20). Whether this requirement is a reward or punishment, we don't know. When your momma called for you when you were a child, you didn't know if she had something good or bad for you. If you have negative faith, fear and guilt, you thought she was calling to admonish or punish. If you are a good child, you usually came running because Mama might let you lick the icing spoon as she frosted a cake.

God called Adam after sin had entered the Garden, and Adam hid. When God called Samuel he answered, *"Here am I Lord."* The righteous, the just do not fear the voice of God, nor do they fear His call-- even the calling of the soul home.

As with God our Father, hopefully we have right relationship and when He calls it's a good calling home, but that soul in Luke was required from a fool who had sought to amass goods and wealth for himself. Take a lesson, God doesn't like the greedy, or hoarders.

Sometimes God may require a person's soul because they are abusing it, or they are hurting others too much. God's thoughts are not ours. Although we do aspire to Godly Wisdom, sometimes God may require a soul because of bad things person might do in the future based on who and where they are now and their lack of repentance.

Or God may require and call the soul home to keep that soul from devastation, hurt, or eternal loss. His ways and thoughts are higher than ours.

All the Earth Lord is full of your Mercy.

The Soul Has Value

The soul has great value. God's plan is that the soul prospers from faith to faith and glory to glory. God wants to increase your mind and help you have righteous and holy Will. He wants to restore your emotions and prosper you financially and physically. He will do it if your soul is prospering. Now you know how to not be refused when asking God, health and financial questions.

... Then shall they give every man a ransom for his soul unto the Lord.... (Exodus 30:12)

... Because my soul was precious in thine eyes this day

(1 Samuel 26:21)

Think of your soul as a seed that's planted in your body. It's a small thing. But it is put there to prosper. How do you prosper it? Feed and water it with the Word, the things of God and the presence of God by study, discipline, worship, and cultivating the Fruits of the Spirit.

God places you with people and in situations and circumstances to see how you will do. Next year, He may present the same tests with different faces to see how you do. If you handle things better, in a more godly way, then you pass the test and get promoted. If you get promoted, then you get more and different tests later on. The tests are never over as long as you are on Earth.

Man is so strange and that he nurtures the intellect in a structured environment for up to 20 years, in some cases--, school. Comparatively, the Spirit man gets little structured training, only about 3 hours a week at church. The emotions are ignored until someone acts out in a way that indicates that they are screaming in mental anguish, emotional pain, physical violence, crime or nervous breakdown. Until something like that happens, people are told to *get over it—to just get over whatever is bothering them.*

The will is nurtured only as a function of what you yourself do. Most people try to break your will to make it like the world's instead of encouraging the building up of a godly will. The will is tested as part of the soul prosperity, and God gives us health and success here on Earth, as we grow our little soul seed into something fit to be presented back to Him.

Like one of the three that given Talents (Matthew 25:15), the soul can be ignored and presented back to God just the same way it was given by doing the following.

- We can avoid people in situations to protect our emotions.
- We can cover up how we really feel about situations.
- We can be with people and be fakes, or
- We can make people allow us to stay emotionally young and immature all of our lives by using sympathy and getting away with guilt, witchcraft, or other demonic techniques.

In any of these ways, the soul remains as it was, unless it regresses by getting worse. I don't know how that could happen, except a person reverts to a newborn baby's behavior. In that case, if you are God, you require that soul of the user yourself before they completely ruin it.

But like the other with the three Talents it can be increased somewhat, which will please God somewhat.

The best outcome is that we strive to prosper our souls, entering into tests, willingly and obediently, searching out the Word, learning the lessons, showing ourselves approved, rightly dividing the Word. In so doing, we pass those tests to arrive at the next level. It's then that we ascend to the next place in God and so on until we are well-pleasing to the Father.

Don't you want God to say over you as He said over Jesus, as He reached the Christ anointing?

This is my beloved son, in whom I am well pleased,

(Matthew 3:17b)

I Got Soul

It was a great day when the Black man came to know he had a soul. James Brown of R&B fame gave a word of knowledge so to speak, when he declared, I got soul. This revelation was not Super Bad, as the self-proclaimed Godfather of Soul said. No, it was super good. Having come from slave days where the Black man was told he was not even human or completely human, hearing *I got soul* was a revelation of God, a light into the mind of the then American Negro.

Soul Control

We must learn to know when the soul is under attack and if all or parts of it has been taken over, or if it has been completely stolen. Or like slavery of so many cultures over time, history repeats itself.

The soul's mind, intellect and emotions if not not operating properly or under the control and authority of the owner and Christ, the soul is under soul control. The 1960s term for this was brainwashed. That means thinking thoughts or thinking the way that another desires you to think or programmed or indoctrinated you to think. Thinking on negative or simple things that you really don't want to think on eats away at the will and can lead to soul control. Sin and its bondages work on the mind first, then sooner or later the body follows. A person could give the control of their soul over to the devil by doing devil-inspired things. If the devil says look at this, you'll like it, don't look. Of course you will like it. The devil knows what to use to tempt you. It's when you look, that you risk losing control of your own soul, even incrementally, to the devil. You may think, I'll just look this one time, then I'll stop. But it doesn't work like that. Even if your body doesn't follow immediately to actually do the sin, the mind is still not in your full control, and your Will is eroded.

You don't want anyone else running your external life, do you? So you must run your own inner life. You must control your own soul, else what's running your inner life will run your external life.

Not having full control over one's emotions is also loss of soul control. Overacting to life's situations may be evidence of someone or something else having soul control over you. Underreacting to situations because of a what's-the-use mentality is also soul control which has been exerted over you by others/entities, usually for the purposes of behavior management.

For example, you have a real response to an event that it causes grief, hurt, heartache or a fight with people you love or care about. So the next time that thing happens, you control yourself--, not fully expressing yourself just to keep the peace. That's being controlled too. The person causing you not to respond the way you should or normally would is controlling you.

Soul Patrol

But you can get your soul back. The Good Shepherd is on soul patrol. He makes a promise that He will restore. So the Holy Spirit, all of God's agents in the Earth, are on soul patrol for your benefit and wholeness. Jesus wants each of us to have whole souls and to be in possession of our souls, else He wouldn't have said in the Word that He restores our soul.

I'm Back

The revelation that the Black man has a soul came over 50 years ago. Now he is fully responsible for it again. Non-Blacks, don't rejoice, repent if your people are the ones that taught the suppressive doctrine to the Negro slaves else, that which you measured out may be returned to you spiritually.

Now we know what a soul is, where it comes from, that we've got one, and why the devil wants it. You know *why* the devil wants it. Now it's time to understand prosperity of the soul. It's time to *understand* why you want and need your soul to prosper and why God cares about it.

Soul Power

The R&B artist James Brown also sung about soul power and said that he had to have it. If only people knew that they really have soul power. Not the ability to wear huge afros, platform shoes and say soulful things when not grooving on the dance floor, but that the soul has real power. This is why the devil wants to steal your soul, because your soul has power.

Soul Power

You move things around in the natural with your physical body, using power and force to lift, carry and build, for example. Regarding *unseen* things, your soul is what you use to move things around and cause things to happen. Your emotions, Will and intellect move mountains, spiritual objects, and obstacles. It draws people, finances, favor and opportunities to you for your success and to God's glory. If you're in full control of your vessel and using it properly for godly purposes it can be very attractive, or it repels the same if you're out of control emotionally, especially. Your reactions, responses, and behavior may cause your own demise or irreparable damage to yourself and others. That's soul power.

Soul Prosperity

Our souls are on loan (of sorts) from God. He is trusting us like the three with the Talents to prosper it. Of course, the one who doubled the amount of Talents is the best and most desired outcome. But, first of all, are you saved? In your spirit, yes, but are you saved in your--

- **Emotions?**
- **Intellect?** And
- **Will?**

What in the world am I talking about, saved in my emotions, saved in my intellect and in my Will? I thought when I got saved, all of me was saved once and for all. Do I have to worry daily whether I'm saved or not?

No; your spirit is regenerated. However, the Word says that we are to choose blessings or cursings—daily. *Choose ye this day* (Deuteronomy 28), implies **daily**. The Devil will torment you with that question over and again. Once saved you're still saved unless you decide to willfully do something heinous against God, don't repent and have no plans of repenting. You can be saved spiritually, but your soul still needs to be trained, directed, and disciplined. The spirit is regenerated, but the soul and the flesh need work.

God regenerates the spirit, then gives **you** authority over the rest of you. That's what perfecting of the saints is all about. That's what working out your salvation with fear and trembling is all about. It's not about dressing it up, it's about stripping it down and making it right and righteous.

Emotions of the Soul

We saw the anguish of the soul.

Genesis 42:21

Some of the emotions of the soul are discouragement, (Numbers 21:4), bitterness. (1Samuel 1:10) and weariness. Job 10:1 tells us that God has every soul in His hand; which includes yours.

In whose hand is the soul of every living thing and the breadth of all mankind? Job 12:10

Are you saved in your emotions?

What makes you angry? Anything? Everything? What do you do when angry? Whom do you hate? Do you spend time being mad at people, or feeling hurt or sorry for yourself? Or do you spend time using your emotions as Jesus used His? He had compassion toward people, but He wasn't always "nice." He certainly wasn't a pushover. He became angry with the Money Changers in the Temple, (Matthew 21:12). The Bible says be angry, but sin not. We know Jesus was sin free, so it's not a sin to throw Money Changers out of the Temple.

Jesus wept more than once. He went to weddings. He had joy, but He kept his focus on His purpose for coming here. So whatever your emotions, if they distract you from what God put you here to do, the devil is succeeding by influencing your soul.

You may be restored in your emotions, will and or intellect by the Ministry of Jesus the Good Shepherd. He is on soul patrol. Study and meditate on Psalm 23, especially verse 3.

Intellect

Are you saved in your intellect? What do you think about on the average day? God knew that you would need some help in your thought life. That's why He's provided Scriptures that say, *think on these things,* (Philippians 4:8), and cast down imagination (2 Corinthians 10:5). God knew that you would have temptations and that you would have to discipline your mind. He tells you to keep your mind stayed on Him, (Isaiah 26:3). The Will is tested to see if you can resist the foolish thoughts presented to the mind or give in to the mind's dictates.

Will

Saved in your Will goes *past* your thinking. Past the thinking is the Will to sin or not sin? What do you purpose to do from moment to moment? Are you wishing you could commit some immoral or sinful deeds? Have you planned some sins you'd like to do and get away with?

Or are you planning in your Will to do the will of the Father? Jesus said, ***"I only do what I see my Father do."*** If that's you, then you are saved in your Will, even if sometimes you will to do one thing, but it doesn't happen quite that way or doesn't happen at all. At least you are *trying* to align your Will with the Father's will.

One way to train your will is to resist very little things first. Then resisting bigger things will be easy. Prosper in your will by resisting temptation. You know those things you shouldn't do. If you can't resist the soda and the chips resist one of them, have the chips with the water or just the soda.

Health & Wealth

Your emotions are reflected in your heart, and your heart is reflected in your emotions. Out of the abundance of the heart, the mouth speaks. Actions speak louder than words. Where your heart is, so is your treasure. Where your treasure is, so is your money. Don't you keep going back to the bank where your money is? Depositing, withdrawing, and checking balances? Why do you keep going back there? Your treasure is there. Where you put your money is where your thought life will be. If you are buying pornography, you'll be thinking on it. If you're spending your money on your timeshare or vacation home, it's simple, you will be thinking about how you want to golf, fish, surf or swim.

Are you saved in your money? Are you saved enough to handle money, are you saved enough to have money at all? This may be why God is refusing you. Some theologians and teachers describe not having money as not having met the criteria to *receive*. I say God, in His infinite Wisdom and Mercy will refuse you for your own good.

Haven't you ever received something that seemed like a good thing, but later it caused you trouble or even torment? Have you ever felt or thought you would have been better off if you hadn't received it?

Or you may look back at your behavior and actions and find that there was no flaw in how you handled that blessing. The so-called blessing itself was the problem. The false blessing wasn't by God's hand, was it? No, it was by man's hand, by the intervention, or the intellect of man, or even the devil.

God knows what you need and when you need it. When you show Him that you're ready, He will provide. Just as when you ask spiritual questions, God provides the answer, usually in the form of a teacher. When you call for physical, tangible goods, God will answer your real need--, when you're ready.

Money

Finding money, such as in a lost wallet with identification but not returning it, is stealing. A saved person who has prospered in their soul would not keep a wallet with the owner's name and address in it, no matter how tempting. But those who may have done this need to know they can be forgiven.

Keeping too much change at the market, for instance, as though you got over--, if that's how you think God has blessed you, that's rather pitiful. We serve a big God. He can find a better way to bless you, and He can find a bigger way to bless you, too. Crumbs from the table are for the unsaved, that $0.29 at the cashier is short in her register, because you have it is not blessing you. That $5 bill she gave you thinking it was a dollar bill, is coming out of her paycheck. God has bigger and better ways to bless you.

The Holy Spirit sees all. He's on soul patrol. He sees what you're doing, what choices you're making spiritually and socially. You know, the Holy Spirit, the part of the Godhead that brings all things to your remembrance. If He can do that, He's got a pretty good memory.

Additionally, if you think a rolling wheel is going to bless you in the gambling hall, then you believe in chance. You have established that wheel is your idol *god*. If you're waiting for gambling to bless you, God won't. God's Kingdom does not work by chance. Saved people shouldn't believe in automated, automatic spinning wheels and slot machines. God has better ways to bless you.

Shoplifting includes changing price tags on items and may also include putting masking tape on the bottom of a brand-new pair of pumps, wearing them to CHURCH on Sunday, then taking them back for full refund on Monday. It definitely includes taking things out of the store that you haven't paid for, no matter what the reason for taking it. It may include taking things out of the store that you've charged on your credit card that you have no intention of paying. Saved people don't shoplift.

God has better ways to bless you.

God does not bless by giving bank robbery schemes. That is obvious stealing and robbery. That is not Wisdom from above, (James 3:15-17). Well, you may say there are no banks in the Bible. There are no commandments against robbing banks. So it's OK to do it? Of course not. If man decided it was OK to rob banks on Wednesday and Friday as long as you're male and at least 25 years of age, would you do it? And God does not give lucky Lotto numbers because Lotto is not of God; it is ruled over by an idol *god*. Being saved in your money takes Wisdom, knowledge, love, discipline, and conscious effort to do what is right and pleasing to God.

God has better ways to bless you.

Whoredoms

The lust for money is ruled over by the *spirit of whoredoms* which is ruled over by Asmodeus the same idol "*god*" that rules over lotto, gambling and such. Don't waste your time and God's time involving Him in prayers for luck, sweepstakes and contests, prizes. You're praying to the wrong God. Our God does not bless that kind of stuff.

> Now the works of the flesh… Are these, Adultery, fornication, uncleanness, lasciviousness, idolatry, witchcraft, hatred, variance, emulations, wrath, strife, seditions, heresies, envyings, murders, drunkenness, revellings, and such like… They that do such things shall not inherit the Kingdom of God.
> (Galatians 5:19-23)

Who Makes You Sick?

Your own emotions can make you sick. Really. God can't prosper your health, for instance, if you are working against Him and yourself by working your flesh. Scriptures say the greater one is in you, but whichever one are you letting have control and influence, or even possession over you will win. If you're a sinner in the world, then the Devil will win your soul. Illness comes along with that. (Who sinned that man or his parents?)

These curses pass down into your generations. Prosperity in your soul means health and having godly emotions. It means having a healthy mind with healthy, godly thoughts and having a godly will.

"I do what I see the Father do, (John 5:19). *I say only what I hear the Father say,"* says Jesus.

Don't refuse me, Lord.

Even if you are saved and Spirit-filled, the Greater One is in you. God can be victorious for you, through you, and in your life. It's completely your choice.

How can I be sure I'm saved in my emotions? And how can my emotions prosper? I want my emotions to be an asset to me, not a liability. The Good Shepherd is on soul patrol, and He will restore your soul.

He restoreth my soul (Psalm 23:3a)

Don't refuse me, Lord. Then allow your soul to prosper. **Make** your soul prosper if you have to, but you must have soul prosperity so you can be in health and prosper financially. Amen.

Tend Your Soul

The gardens round, yet not fenced about.
The workers toil their fruit, has not
Yet found its season
And some here reason,
This toiling takes too long.

So some who sit amid the rows
And give a song about their woes
And some who take to taking drink
While lazy ones, they sit and think
Of other ways to reap the fruit.
Harvest seeds; bring home the loot.
Yet in the day of setting sun,
They have no fruit, not even one.
And some decide that this is too hard
And take to working a smaller yard.
Exchange their plot, their land, their piece

For a smaller place, to work with ease.

They work a while, a half a day.

They work half-hearted, half the way,

Then find the growth from exchanged seeds

Were rapid-growing, fruitless weeds.

While those who toiled full by the rules,

Which they learned in life's own schools;

And spent the time by days in whole,

Had tended well their very souls.

Dr. Marlene Miles, 1991

Exercise:

28. Is my soul prospering?

Compare when you first became saved to five years ago, and to this time last year. To see if you are prospering in your soul. Or compared to right now, if you've not been saved at least five years.

29. Intellect. What do I think about?

Well, what do I set out to accomplish or do on my daily spiritual and natural life?

30. What have I resisted lately? That I would in the past have given in to. Thoughts. Foods. Habits. Activities.

31. Emotions do I have godly emotions or demonic emotions? (Galatians 5:19-21).

32. Treasure- Is my money saved. Spiritually speaking.

33. Time- What am I doing with my time? Am I doing sad things?

34. Talent- How am I using my gifts and talents to further the Kingdom of God? Or have I separated the good for the world and giving what's left over to God?

Thank you for purchasing this volume, we pray for your complete prosperity of your soul so that you may be in health and increase financially, in the name of Jesus.

Amen—.

Dear Reader:

Thank you for acquiring and reading this book. I pray it has blessed you and that you will be even more prosperous and healthy in your life.

Shalom,

Dr. Marlene Miles

Enjoy Bible teaching and messages on the Dr. Miles YouTube Channel.

Find spiritual warfare prayers on the Warfare Prayer Channel on YouTube.

Prayerbooks by this author

While most books by this author have prayer points either throughout the book or at the end, there are some books that are only prayers. You just open up the book and pray. They are listed below:

Prayers Against Barrenness: *For Success in Business and Life*

Fruit of the Womb: *Prayers Against Barrenness*

Beauty Curses, *Warfare Prayers Against*
https://a.co/d/5Xlc20M

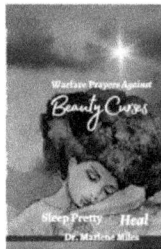

Courts of Marriage: Prayers for Marriage in the Courts of Heaven *(prayerbook)*
https://a.co/d/cNAdgAq

Courtroom Warfare @ Midnight *(prayerbook)*
https://a.co/d/5fc7Qdp

Demonic Cobwebs *(prayerbook)* https://a.co/d/fp9Oa2H

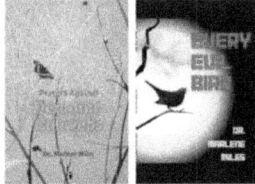

Every Evil Bird https://a.co/d/hF1kh1O

Gates of Thanksgiving

Spirits of Death, Hell & the Grave, Pass Over Me and My House

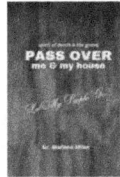

Throne of Grace: Courtroom Prayer

Warfare Prayer Against Poverty
https://a.co/d/bZ611Yu

Other books by this author

AK: The Adventures of the Agape Kid

Already Married in the Spirit: *Why You May Not Be Married in the Natural*

AMONG SOME THIEVES

Do Not Swear by the Moon

Don't Refuse Me, Lord (4 book series)

https://a.co/d/idP34LG

Dream Defilement

The Emptiers: *Thieves of Darkness, 1*
https://a.co/d/5I4n5mc

Evil Touch

Failed Assignment

Fantasy Spirit Spouse https://a.co/d/hW7oYbX

FAT Demons (The): *Breaking Demonic Curses*
https://a.co/d/4kP8wV1

The Fold (5-book series)

- The Fold (Book 1)
- Name Your Seed (Book 2)
- The Poor Attitudes of Money (3)
- Do Not Orphan Your Seed (4)
- For the Sake of the Gospel (5)
- My Sowing Journal

Gang Ups: Touch Not God's Anointed

Getting Rid of Evil Spiritual Food

https://a.co/d/i2L3WYQ

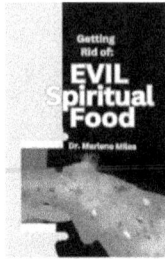

got HEALING? Verses for Life

got LOVE? Verses for Life

got HOPE? Verses for Life

got money? https://a.co/d/g2av41N

How to Dental Assist

How to Dental Assist2: Be Productive, Not Wasteful

How to STOP Being a Blind Witch or Warlock

I Take It Back

Legacy

Let Me Have A Dollar's Worth
https://a.co/d/h8F8XgE

Level the Playing Field

Living for the NOW of God

Lose My Location https://a.co/d/crD6mV9

Love Breaks Your Heart

Made Perfect In Love

Man Safari, *The*

Marriage Ed. Rules of Engagement & Marriage

Made Perfect in Love

Money Hunters: Beware of Those

Money on the Altar https://a.co/d/4EqJ2Nr

Mulberry Tree, *The* https://a.co/d/9nR9rRb

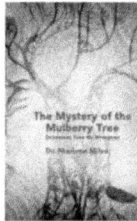

Motherboard (The) - *Soul Prosperity Series*

Name Your Seed

Occupy: *Until I Return*

Plantation Souls

Players Gonna Play

Power Money: Nine Times the Tithe

https://a.co/d/gRt41gy

The Power of Wealth *(forthcoming)*

Powers Above

The Robe, Part 1, The Lessons of Joseph

The Robe, Part II, The Lessons of Joseph

Seasons of Grief

Seasons of Waiting

Seasons of War

Second Marriage, Third~~, *Any Marriage*
https://a.co/d/6m6GN4N

Sift You Like Wheat

Six Men Short: What Has Happened to all the Men?

Soul Prosperity soul prosperity series 3
https://a.co/d/5p8YvCN

Souls Captivity soul prosperity series 2

The Spirit of Anti-Marriage

The Spirit of Poverty

StarStruck

SUNBLOCK

The Swallowers: *Thieves of Darkness*, 3

Take It Back

This Is NOT That: How to Keep Demons from Coming at You

Time Is of the Essence

Too Many Wives: *Why You Have Lady Problems*

Tormenting Spirits   https://a.co/d/dAogEJf

Toxic Souls

Triangular Power *(series)*

- Powers Above
- SUNBLOCK
- Do Not Swear by the Moon
- STARSTRUCK

Unbreak My Heart: *Don't Let Me Die*

Uncontested Doom

Unguarded Hours, *The*

Unseen Life, *The* (forthcoming)

Upgrade: How to Get Out of Survival Mode

- Toxic Souls (Book 2 of series)
- Legacy (Book 3 of series)

The Wasters: *Thieves of Darkness,* Bk 2
https://a.co/d/bUvI9Jo

What Have You to Declare? What Do You Have With You from Where You've Been?

When I Was A Child, *I Prayed As a Child*

When the Devourer is Rebuked

https://a.co/d/1HVv8oq

The Wilderness Romance *(series)* This series is about conducting a Godly relationship and marriage with someone who is a Wilderness person. It is about how to recognize it and navigate through it. These books are about how not to get caught up in such.

- *The Social Wilderness*
- *The Sexual Wilderness*
- *The Spiritual Wilderness*

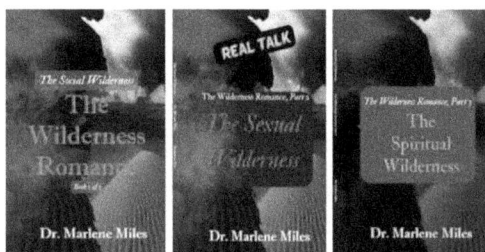

Other Series

The Fold (a series on Godly finances) https://a.co/d/4hz3unj

Soul Prosperity Series https://a.co/d/bz2M42q

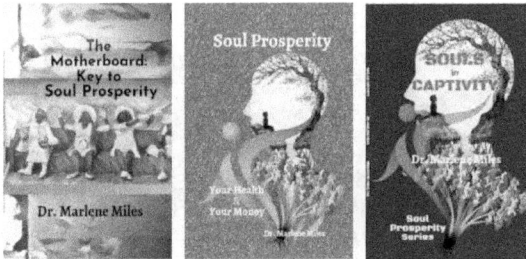

Spirit Spouse books

https://a.co/d/9VehDSo

https://a.co/d/97sKOwm

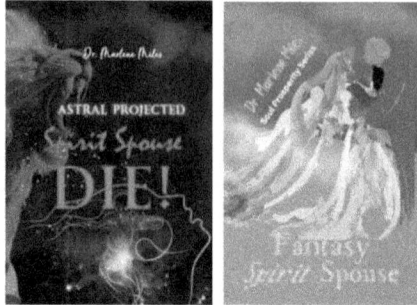

Battlefield of Marriage, The

https://a.co/d/eUDzizO

Players Gonna Play

https://a.co/d/2hzGw3N

Matters of the Heart

Made Perfect in Love https://a.co/d/70MQW3O

Love Breaks Your Heart https://a.co/d/4KvuQLZ

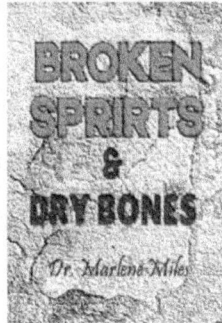

Unbreak My Heart https://a.co/d/84ceZ6M

Broken Spirits & Dry Bones https://a.co/d/e6iedNP

Thieves of Darkness series

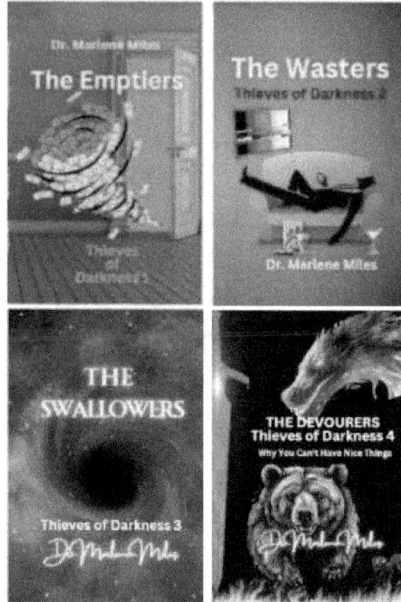

The Emptiers https://a.co/d/heio0dO

The Wasters https://a.co/d/5TG1iNQ

The Swallowers https://a.co/d/1jWhM6G

The Devourers: Why We Can't Have Nice Things
https://a.co/d/87Tejbf

Triangular Powers https://a.co/d/aUCjAWC

Upgrade (series) *How to Get Out of Survival Mode*
https://a.co/d/aTERhX0

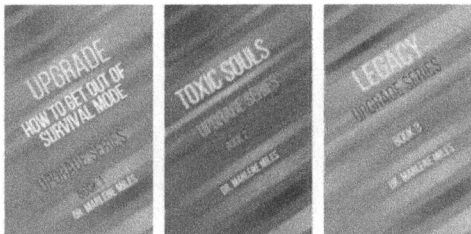

www.ingramcontent.com/pod-product-compliance
Lightning Source LLC
LaVergne TN
LVHW051419080426
835508LV00022B/3162